# Bella Grande

*Nicola Sellars*

All money made from the sale of this book will be donated to Penny Brohn UK, to help people live well with cancer.

Cover artwork: Miche Watkins

# INTRODUCTION

*By Claire Williamson and Sarah Bird*

I initially met Nicki in 2004 at the Bristol Cancer Help Centre, where Fiona Hamilton and I were facilitating a therapeutic creative writing group. Poetry was already part of Nicki's life, and I think the poem 'Big Good' had already been written. Nicki would regularly come to Can Openers (a poetry reading open floor) at Bristol Central Library with others from the Cancer Help Centre group. Over time we formed a friendship and discovered that we also had mutual friends. Our affinity grew and Nicki became a godmother to my daughter, Sophia, and shared the love of our schnauzer, Milly.

Nicki and I often spoke about poetry and she'd sometimes ask me to edit her poems. For this reason, it felt natural to work on the poems for her collection that Nicki had nominated – in fact she left notes on some poems, like *needs work*, or *could be two poems?*

The editing process was mainly pruning and shaping the pieces to show off their best selves. It has been a privilege, which has allowed me to hold Nicki close and changed me in the process. I hope you feel the same when you read *Bella Grande. – Claire*

Nicki and I met in the local dog park, through the aforementioned schnauzer, Milly, and my lurcher, Flash. I was going through breast cancer treatment at the time – Nicki understood how it felt to have 'chemo fog' and no hair.

Just weeks before she died, she asked if Claire and I would put together a book of her poems. In preparation, I read the 'About the Author' section from her novel, *Colour Me In*. The last line reads as follows: *She hopes one day to publish a collection of poetry*. Better late than never, dear Nicki. I hope we have done you justice. *– Sarah*

## Bella Grande

credevo che niente di grande potrebbe mai succedere a me

sicuramente non bella grande come vincere la lotteria
ma neanche brutta grande
non ero abbastanza
non ero abbastanza niente
troppo ordinaria
le cose grande succedono agli altri,
mai a me
la mia vita è una vita molto normale
non succede mai niente di straordinario

quindi per forza il nodulo dovev'essere un niente
una ciste, niente di niente

invece ho sbagliato,
non era niente
era qualcosa di grande,
brutta grande,
è successo a me,
proprio a me!

ma sai una cosa?
una cosa bella grande?

quando mi è successo questa cosa brutta grande
cominciavano a succedere
tante cose belle piccole:
telefonate
cartoline
abbracci
comprensioni
amicizie
amori

poi c'era tempo
tempo per riposare e riflettere
per parlare
per scrivere
per capire

tante tante piccole cose belle
che insieme
diventavano
una cosa bella grande
molto bella, molto grande

fino a diventare…
dopo tanto tempo
dopo tanti anni
…più grande
della cosa brutta grande
che non avrei mai pensato potesse succedere
proprio a me.

**Big Good**

I didn't think anything big
could ever happen to me,
certainly not big good like
winning the lottery.

But not big bad either,
I wasn't enough,
not enough of anything,
really ordinary,
big things only happen
to other people,
not to me.

Therefore the lump
had to be nothing,
a cyst, a nothing of nothing.

But I was wrong,
it wasn't nothing,
it was something,
something big,
something big bad,
and it happened to me!

But I'll tell you something,
something big good.

When the big bad thing happened,
lots of little good things,
started to happen,
telephone calls,
cards,
hugs,
understanding,
friendship,
love.

Then there was time,
time to rest and think,
time to speak,
time to write and
time to understand.

Lots and lots of little good things,
which together
became,
a big good thing,
very big, very good.

Until it became,
after a long time,
after many years,
much bigger,
than the big bad thing,
I never thought
could happen to me!

# CONTENTS

Ward A604
Peace

## CANCER

First Diagnosis
Painting Myself
Gaia
Life Threatening
Mary
Recovering the Sass
Pomegranate Seed
Scraped Bare
Treasure Hunt

## LETTING GO

Letting Go
Mid Winter
Silhouette
Too Late
The Flames Within

# BEING

## Certainty

We seek it in the tone of our loved ones' voices
in the hand-holding, the comforting glances.

Sifting and sorting, we want to base our life on it:
What will happen? How will things turn out?

Elusive –
we'll never know it, even when we believe we do.

Would life smell sweet?
Is knowing always knowing?
Living really living?

Or is that sudden call,
the fork in the road,
the anxious wait
what we need to get our blood pumping
to feel really alive?

## Circling

In the frosty park
we circle.

Watchful, but noisy
as feet crunch winter ground.

Heads turn towards
each other, not quite facing.

Like dogs who sniff and run away,
returning to sniff and flit again.

Once we were silent and stealthy.
Now strained, like frosted grass, we snap
this beautiful fragility.

## Colour Me

Colour my walls and floor
with earth and sand.
Colours, to ground me,
to hold me down,
so I don't float away.

Colour my words with
strong flames,
orange and red
to fire me up, so I have
the energy to transform.

Colour my sleeping
with hues of lavender,
to softly waft me
to a land
where I can be at peace.

Colour my reawakening
with blues of the sky
and turquoise of the sea,
so I can be washed
clean, in my renewal.

Colour my knowing
with honey and lime
so the time to taste
this bitter, sweet life
does not pass me by.

## Gran

Bittersweet the link
between love and death,
death and love.
Her grasp no longer strong,
her breath no longer
free, she dies.

She leaves love hanging
in the air.
I can almost touch it,
but it turns to water.

The bread doesn't rise
as it did when she made it.

Something in those
brown veined hands
in that firm, life-grasping
hold, that I don't have.

## Just Being

Have you ever felt
that drainy feeling
when you can't get out of bed?

Have you ever felt
that desperate need to stop
the voices in your head?

Have you ever wished
you could just go away
and shut it all right out?

Or run to the top
of a very high hill
and shout and shout and shout?

I've been dreaming a lot
about a desert island,
a place where there's only me.

A place where I just
sit and stare and sit
and stare and be and be and be.

A place where doing
doesn't matter,
it's who I am, that does.

Have you ever wondered
why just being,
is so hard for us?

## Pink Grasses
*for Meena*

The long pink grasses rustle their music,
a deathly secret, whispered in your voice.
A voice that came out of the smallness of you,
liquid power cascading in waves round the world.

From bright eyes you sparkled down to your toes,
with a love of life that infected us all.
I live with your voice rustling in my pink grasses
and fragments of your sparkle in my eyes.

## My Love is Here
*for Rachel and Jeremy*

I promise to chase the shadows away
and listen to you whisper in the dark.

I promise to show you a rainbow
and bask with you in the sunshine.

I promise to walk beside you,
to keep your footsteps sure,
over the mountain path
and along the boulevard.

I will carry your bags
and you will carry mine.

I will try to talk when it's hard to talk
and to listen when it's hard to listen.
I will hold you when you cry.
When you laugh, I will laugh with you.

These heartfelt promises
come from a place of love.
The place where hands intertwine
and eyes meet.
Where the heart quickens
and the smile grows inside.
Where the warmth rises and I know
'my love is here.'

# CREATING

## Baby Love

I love babies,
the folded petals
of their personalities
waiting to flower open,
bursting out sometimes
when they cry
and every sinew
of their little red bodies
strains to communicate.

I love the small softness,
the sometimes sweetness,
even the sick and pooh smell
that is uniquely baby.

Watching them in their
first few weeks
as their eyes begin
to focus, fixing
intently on you,
drinking you in,
absorbing you totally.

And, returning their gaze,
you find magic,
a magnetic force
that draws you in
and flutters joy in your heart,
as you fall in love.

## Lacey Knickers

I'm going to wear
my lacey knickers.

Yes. I know –
a little racey for me.
I'm normally a comfy
nicely turned out,
firmly on the shelf,
encase my bum in soft-cotton girl.

Racey kick-arse lacey knickers
I'm gonna kick arse today.

## Music*

Winding its way from the background of life –
a way of coping, a way out of pain and stifling sorrow –
releasing tears, imprisoned fears.

And lifting spirits – whatever speaks to your soul?
Folk, Blues, Jazz, Rock'n'Roll?
The accompaniment of my life.

*The last disc in Nicki's CD player was Miles Davis' *Kind of Blue*

## Out of my Dressing Gown

I'm out of my dressing gown today.
The sky is full of angel's wings,
maybe today will be okay.

The tight grip on the top of my head
is looser. The furrows in my brow
not so deep. Maybe tonight I will sleep.

I'll walk in proper steps, not slipper-shuffle.
Put on make-up, brush my hair,
sit in a chair, not slump on the bed.

I saw the sky. It's full of angel's wings.
I'm not ready to fly but,
I'm out of my dressing gown today.

By what miracle did my hands undo
that soft tie belt? By what miracle
did I pull my arms from those sleeves?

The tightness of clothes encases my skin,
leaning towards the door. I may put on shoes,
walk in proper steps with the sky full of angel's wings.

## Poetry

In a dark cave, waits
a not yet shape.

Fragments of ideas
loosely held together
by a vision, unclear.
Mixed emotions,
vying for position.

The fragments are broken.
Separate, put together differently –
rippled through with another vision,
the echoes of emotion, sometimes dark
sometimes light.

Until at a specific moment,
predefined, or spontaneous,
that not yet shape becomes form

and leaves the cave,
into light trembling newness.

## The River

The water on the table top is turning
to ice and chills my fingers as they
trace it into a river.

The river is wide and welcoming
as our boat chugs along, the sun warm
on my bare shoulders,
casting our shadows on the water.

Heavy on my shoulders, call the plumber,
clean the floor. But I am still,
a frozen figure
tracing a river on a table top.

Children wave from the shore
as our boat passes bamboo huts,
bobbing houseboats, and families
mending nets on the sand.

There is a blueness to my skin,
a numbness in my solitude.
I cannot move.

Mooring aside a blue painted boat
we exchange melons and bananas
for fish and bread.
Sharing wine and laughter.

The children play chase, jumping from
shore to boat, to boat, to shore. And then,
I see them, in the impish smiles and
wide brown laughing eyes.

The broken pipe drips steady.
I am ice in my kitchen
and they are gone.

**The Missed Train**

Shrouded in a choking cloud
the train pulled away without her.
The girls chattering at the back of the hall
missed being moved by her call to arms:
*Women are citizens too*
*we should have the vote by rights*
*instead we have to fight for it.*
The man from the local paper
waiting outside the hall
missed interviewing her.
She missed looking up at him,
seeing something in his dark eyes.
She missed his invitation to dinner
a conversation of like minds.
She missed invitations to other meetings.
She missed a long lost friend
come to reignite their acquaintance.
She missed the train
but has no idea what she really missed.

**Willow Tree Barn**

Wood is warm,
homely, soft light,
smooth to the touch,
almost yielding.

This light wood-home,
wood floors, doors and
beams, proudly still
displaying its past-life.

High-roofed barn
opened and made light,
multiple windows,
spacious, but cosy.

Honey-wood wrapping
keeping safe, contained
family sounds, family love
and family pain.

# DAD

## A Spot in the Brain

*As a little boy I tried*
*to ride a bicycle,*
*but kept falling off.*
*My parents despaired*
*of me, ran behind me,*
*couldn't stop me falling.*

A flicker of recognition
at the mention of a name?
It has spread out from
a spot in the brain.

*When my father died*
*they gave me a huge*
*tin of Quality Street.*
*I was seven, I didn't*
*know why. Then they*
*took me to see him.*

## No

An alien has taken over my father's body
snuffled out the bright light and shine,
crushed the sense of humour,
killed the memory,
sucked the life out of him,
turned him into a
shadowed corpse,
until every last spark of the
man has gone:

No bright eyes light
No warm smile
No bad taste jokes
No corny memories
No life left.

The man has gone,
he has been going
for a long time.

**Silver Stars**
*for Dad*

After you died, night crouched like a panther.
Bitter tongue-taste, lungs ached, heart stone-heavy.

You took the silver stars with you,
they are the tears running down my skin.

You took the laughter.
Remorse hangs in my breath.
You took the silver stars with you.

## The Lost Photo

Light bounces off a red bauble
reflecting our happy smiles.

Me with my curly perm
and shoulder-padded dress.
You with dark grey hair and
Life-sparkling eyes.
An Eighties Christmas.

Glasses held up to each other in toast,
my eyes blurry with alcohol.
It is the smile I need.

I've searched albums, boxes,
drawers. Opened and shaken books –
all in vain.

I need the smile.
That rare smile caught on film.
Proof of a daughter's love for a father.
Love I was rarely
able to show.

Love I could see
in that Eighties Christmas.

# MUM

## MUM

### In Margot May's

Roses climb the china teacup in my hand.
A baby cries.
My thoughts go to my bright mother
who understands world events,
but forgets to eat.

Skills held for a lifetime, slipping away.
This precious time –
connecting eyes and knowing smiles,
of love for children and grandchildren.

I pray that she will always feel that love,
face spread wide with laughter.

She taught me to love dainty tea sets.
She taught me to love.

The baby held close ceases to cry,
its crumpled face settles into peace.

## Love of Books

Sharp mind, love of books,
nine o'clock curl up, a strong lamp,
armchair dramas – Mum never happier.

I'd pack just one book for my train journey,
knowing I'd arrive at the library –
*Do you want to laugh or cry, or both?*

Recommendations –
exciting new titles she'd been devouring,
favourite authors' works in a row.

She doesn't read anymore,
enjoys being read to – titbits
from poems or children's books.

I've lost my librarian – the one
who kindled my love of books
so many genres, so many adventures.

When I open an old cherished friend,
start a new one – there she is
my supporter, my hand-holder.

## A Picture of You

I drew a picture of you
in chalk on a blackboard.

But it rubbed itself out
bit by bit.

The smile playing around your lips
gradually faded.

The knowing slowly left your eyes
until they looked lost.

The wrinkles didn't go
but became quieter and softer.

The chin lost its defiance
the hands lost their purpose.

The last thing to go though
was that pretend-cross look

you always put on
when someone teased you.

## The Only Colourful Thing on the Rail

*That red suits you,*
you said.
*Warming and cheerful*
*and the fabric is soft.*

Persuaded.
I bought it.
And now it hangs
on the rail
among the blacks
and the browns and the
greys. A bright
reminder of the last time
you and I
went shopping together.

## Ward A604

*The kidnappers have offered me*
*food and water.*
*I have tubes in my nose.*

*Breathe in, they say.*
*Breathe out.*
*They don't tell me*
*which way is in.*

*They've stolen my daughter.*
*They don't tell me where she is.*
*The people around the next bed laugh.*

*There are lots of little connections*
*I try to explain, but the words run out,*
*I don't know how to keep them going.*

*What have you done with her?*
*I want to ask,*
*but the words don't . . .*

## Peace

If I could return to you,
the forgotten memories.
If I could chase shadows away,
bid them never engulf you again,
I would, in an instant.

You once felt my pain,
now I feel yours.
I want to banish fear,
the sense of it, the presence of it,
from your life, forever.

Fear haunted you –
a war child, evacuated
unsafe.

After a lifetime
rising to challenges,
fears conquered,
you deserve peace.

In a tumble of forgetting –
thoughts that won't finish –
and words that won't come –
elusive peace.

# CANCER

**First Diagnosis**

The Italian lady doctor walking away
*Oh yes it's malignant,*
down the corridor
*the x ray showed,*
walking away
*two lumps on your lungs,*
down the corridor
*we can do keyhole surgery,*
walking away
*but first the breast,*
down the corridor
*then the lungs,*
walking away
*see you in the operating theatre,*
down the corridor.

**Painting Myself**

I'm painting myself
orange flowers on my still
voluptuous left breast –

a trellis leading down
to my round stomach –
spreading over the stretch marks
out to the cellulite
maybe bluebells?

A blue streak from my right eye
down my cheek.

*Why?* I hear you cry.
Because –

I'm painting myself

*Why?* I hear you cry.
Because I …
need colour.

When cancer came in
colour went out.

## Gaia

I want to purge my body of disease,
it eats my vital energy to grow.

It re-roots my blood vessels for its own ends.
It ladens my atmosphere with poison

and clogs my rivers and seas
with toxic rubbish, I cannot break down.

Its mission is to grow at any price. I pay
with the life of every living organism in my body.

I will have to give it storms,
so tempestuous it cannot hold on.

I will bring wildfires to rage through its terrain,
giving it nothing to feed on.

I will flood its cells, drowning it
in my own life blood.

I will take back my blood vessels
and clear the poison from my atmosphere.

To rid me of this disease,
I will have to transform myself.

## Life Threatening

I'm learning to take my days gently,
trying not to push them
into any definite shape,
which could give an appearance of certainty.

It would only be appearance
but comforting nevertheless.
A schedule, a pattern to life repeating
and to be counted on.

Illness has released me from the need
to be up at the same hour, ready for work,
but I crave that steady ritual.

We fit ourselves into the shape that life gives us,
the job, the parent, the child,
a template requiring juggling rather than questioning.

When that's removed, questions abound,
how to heal, how to be true to myself?

When life threatening comes along,
the need for flexible days follows
and the appearance of certainty is gone.

I want a list of events that will happen,
of things I can count on so that I can pretend
there is something constant, solid and
unchanging about this life.

## Mary

She comes towards me, fast and fierce.
Her face obscured by a long blue headscarf
matching her robes.
I know who she is.

No time to be afraid,
she's on me, both hands on my shoulders
pushing me so hard I stumble backwards.

Before I can catch breath,
she pushes me again.

*Hey,* I say. Anger rises up inside me and
I push her back.
She pushes me again, and I fight,
grabbing her headscarf.
Slowly it slips off. I am frozen still.
She has my face.

*Fight,* she says, *Rise up from your sofa,*
*dispel all doubt from your mind,*
*and fight for a life that's worth saving.*

**Recovering the Sass**

Once upon a time –
there was a blues-loving
arse-wriggling
sexy-feeling woman with a steely love of life.

Then came along breast cancer,
loss, grief and moved goal posts –
a steroid filled blob took her place.

As time passed –
maybe a small part of her came back,
a little bit of toe-tapping
some smiling, Prosecco drinking.

Then along came a fragile mother –
full of contagious anxiety and depression.
She fought to keep her mother's music playing,
while her own tunes were left unheard...

Time passed and mother
went into the care of others –
slowly exhaustion and anxiety
began to ease.

But as the toe-tapping was about to begin –
she found cancer in her lung,
deep in her bones.

During this time of fear,
overwhelming exhaustion,
she could not hear her own music.

Gradually she reached out for support
and with the help of friends,
she began to find the beat of her own drum.

Dancing to her own rhythm
to keep the cancer quiet.
Forced to retreat in a body breathing in fresh air,
finding her own way.

The steel began to creep back,
as did the blues and the fun
and a little bit of arse-wriggling.

And she knows now that
being her own blues-loving sassy self
is the only way to stay alive.

## Pomegranate Seed

Shock floods through me, an adrenaline rush.
Tears prickle but don't fall.
Here again.
I must have a pomegranate seed
in my mouth.

I had thought, optimistic as ever,
that there was a natural balance.
After bad news comes good,
warm weighs heavier than cold, and
at some point the cancer has to stop growing.
This has become my Odyssey.

Hades' presence is familiar now,
as I grow accustomed to the shadows.
The doctor, seeking words of comfort
is groping in the dark. As am I –

I'm learning to find my way
without light.

## Scraped Bare

Stripped down to the bone.
Scraped and scraped and scraped
starlight white.
As bare as a silver birch in winter.

I have scraped me
down to nothing.

I don't know how to ask
in this nothingness.

## Treasure Hunt

A soldier stumbling from
an explosion.

Walking dazed with no
sense of direction.

There are no posts to guide me,
only cancer markers that
keep rising.

The stench of death is near,
I don't want to breathe it in.

*Baby steps*, a voice whispers.
*Don't try to find the whole map.*

*One street name will do,*
*one number that seems*
*familiar.*

*Lost can become found,*
*clue by clue.*

# LETTING GO

## Letting Go

I hesitate.
I cannot plunge in.

The water surges forward,
without thought,
I remove shoes and socks.

A sharp intake of breath
my toes are in.

A surge rises up from my feet
through legs, torso, arms and head
in an ecstatic ripple.

Wanting more of this energy
I step right in.

The bands around my chest
loosen as breath rushes to my lungs.

The rods that hold my arms and legs rigid,
buckle and bend.

The cold water brings a warmth
I've never known before.

Retreating to return with a renewed force,
it beckons me in.

Unable to resist I surrender,
wading in over my knees.

## Mid Winter

Let me stay in this blanket stillness,
held gently in its folds.

I no longer want to race
through these dark times
into lighter days.

As a child I cried at the carol
*In the Bleak Mid-Winter,*
but now it is not bleak to me.

The soft quiet holds me,
giving me a chance to be still.

## Silhouette

I want to cast a longer shadow,
a tree in the late afternoon, winter sun.
To strip myself down to bare branches,
to stand exposed as the last leaves flutter to the ground.
Honesty to take the breath away,
a state of grace I've hardly dared to dream,
to be lovable.

## Too Late

The ticking of the clock
etches the passing of time
onto the stillness.

If anything scares me,
it is that.

We measure in seconds
and minutes,
the passing of a life.

In the blinking of an eye
it has all ticked away
and what have I done?

I have poems and love
to seek.

I cannot go until I have
found them.

But I don't know where
to look.

Still the clock ticks,
dividing the time
like black lines on a ruler.

## The Flames Within

I closed my eyes
white flames rose from inside me,
unfolding like a flower and reaching up.

The dark pink cancers dripping down,
the pink and grey turning white.
My lungs clean again.

My spine shiny, my ribs clean,
my skull and pelvis not quite,
yet I am cleansed.

The fire cleanses me and new life grows in me.